11

11 Simply Brilliant Ideas for a Life of Love, Joy, and Abundance

Georgette Van Vliet

My intention in writing this book is to share ideas that have helped me achieve the success and life that I love. The concepts are not meant to take the place of medical advice.

Cover, Interior, and eBook design by Steven W. Booth,
www.GeniusBookServices.com

Table of Contents

Dedication

I dedicate this book to everyone I've met, near and far. Every interaction I've had—positive and negative—has helped me grow into the person I am today.

I especially want to thank my husband, Ike; my son, Tommy; and my mom, Argere. We are a team!

Welcome

Dr. Wayne W. Dyer's book, Your Erroneous Zones, ignited my quest to understand myself and what it means to feel fulfilled. His uplifting messages about positive thinking and the notion that we can control our thoughts inspired me to open my mind and heart to a new way of living. It was revolutionary to realize that depression and misery didn't have to be my natural state. I picked up that book more than twenty years ago, and I embarked on a spiritual journey, which has enhanced my life in so many beautiful ways. I am blessed and honored to share this knowledge with you.

I dreamed of having a magnificent life filled with exotic vacations and a beach house in the

Hamptons, but I also wanted to feel content, peaceful, worthy, and confident. Not only was I lacking in all these areas, but I never quite felt like I belonged anywhere. Whether it was amongst my family members, friends, coworkers, or acquaintances, I felt like an outsider—it looked like they had these close relationships, and I somehow didn't fit in. I had this dreariness hanging over me like a rain cloud on a leash. It seemed like everyone else was living an ideal life, and my life was just ***HARD***.

Granted, many of the circumstances of my youth were challenging. My dad moved to Europe when I was thirteen. We were very close, and I was traumatized when he left. Around the same time, my brother became a heroin addict. My mother and I desperately tried to save him from his dangerous lifestyle. He overdosed and died, which left us shocked and heartbroken.

Because of my home life, I had no idea what I was doing when it came to dating. I have had my share of heartbreaks and difficult relationships. I was a sad and lonely person, which isn't the greatest recipe when you're looking for a companion. My first husband was emotionally abusive and caustic. I was unhappy, and even though I ended the marriage, it took me many years to recover. Not only did I move from one extremely unhealthy relationship to another, but I was also making impulsive professional decisions that left me aimless. I didn't recognize the red flags flying everywhere, warning me to slow down and take control of my life. When I met Ike, I knew my life was on the right path. When we married, we were so excited to start a family, but it took five years to conceive our son. Anyone who has experienced infertility understands how awful this is. All you want is a child, which you assume is a natural part of life, and when you don't conceive, you feel angry, frustrated, and frightened. Even though my pregnancy and delivery were perfect, the emotional toll infertility took on me really zapped any vitality I had left.

I felt like I was in a perpetual fog. Other people seemed to have magical, carefree, effortless lives, which didn't seem to be in the cards for me. I never felt like one of the lucky ones, and at no time did it occur to me that I had the power to turn this around. Reading books by spiritual authors gave me hope, inspiration and guidance. I persevered because I deeply believed in this journey. I attended workshops and lectures; I experienced deep, healing bodywork, such as Jin Shin Jitsu and Hellerwork; I practiced yoga and meditation. I was open to learning everything I could on my lifelong quest for vitality and joy.

As I continued to read and explore, I learned about The Law of Attraction* (LOA) through Esther and Jerry Hicks, and Abraham*. LOA was a significant piece of the puzzle that catapulted me into my new abundant life. The premise is that we are constantly attracting whatever we choose to give our attention to whether we realize it or not. This new idea jarred me. I was able to see how my negative thoughts and emotions were creating more negative experiences in my life! For example, if I was feeling like I didn't have enough money, that was the thought I was sending out to

* Terms marked with a star (*) can be found in the glossary on page 133

the universe, and the universe was responding by showing me exactly what I believed - that I don't have enough money!

On the flip side, we have a lot of control over what we think and we can create a wonderful life for ourselves by thinking positive thoughts, which will attract positive experiences into our lives. That has been the most motivating factor in turning my thoughts around and being clear and precise about the messages I project.

LOA teaches us that we have an internal awareness monitor that we can use every day to guide us: our emotions. If we are feeling any negative emotions, right away, we can change those thoughts, which will allow the situation to get better quickly. As we understand and practice these concepts, the easier it will be to attract any of our desires. The more positive our feelings, the faster our desires will come to us.

At the base of creating the life you want is feeling the wonderful emotions—even before your dreams come true. So if you would feel excited to get a $10,000 raise, feel excited now—as if it already happened. If you would feel relaxed and content sitting on the beach in Hawaii, picture it and feel those wonderful feelings right now. When you feel good, you allow better experiences to flow into your life. I was blown away by the simplicity with which I could turn my life around.

As I read Abraham-Hicks books and listened to their CDs, I was intrigued by the notion of *Asking** for what I desired; *Believing** that I could attract my desires into my life, and being open to *Receiving** my manifestations. The concepts sounded wonderful but completely out of my reach. How was I supposed to feel good all the time? I was angry at so many people! How could I overcome all the issues I was carrying around like a sack of rocks up a mountain? Couldn't someone take a glimpse at my bank account to understand my woes? Even though all these resistant thoughts swirled around like an ever-present dust storm, intuitively I believed that positive thinking and the concepts of the Law of Attraction could further assist me in reaching my lofty goals and dreams.

Spiritual literature gave me the perspective to help me make many wonderful changes to my life, but understanding LOA really made the difference. I didn't know how to release the grip my negative behaviors had on me because they were so deeply ingrained. I used to jump out of bed in the morning and rush to get ready to drive to work; I was stressed out, worrying about debt and worrying about my son. I spent the entire day with my hands in fists as I ran around feeling overly responsible to make sure I met deadlines and pleased everyone. The tension in my neck and shoulders was fierce. Sometimes the anxiety and stress were so much that I couldn't breathe. Then I would drive home, exhausted, with no energy to give my family, let alone cook and have a life in the evening. Drained was my middle name.

Slowly, I was able to retrain my thoughts and behaviors, so my life didn't feel like a perpetual emergency. My good friends, Cheryl and Sharon, would send me YouTube links to Esther's workshops, and I listened to them faithfully every morning on my half hour commute to work. At night, I would read excerpts from Esther and Jerry Hicks' books. My days became sprinkled with positive reminders that my life wasn't a disaster. One of the first things I taught myself was how to wake up, smile, and think about how happy I am to have my family. I love my warm, comfortable home. I feel grateful and satisfied. It is such a pleasant way to start my day.

Other aspects of my life became easier. When I used to pay bills, I was angry and resentful at all the expenses and how much money was flowing out. Now when I pay bills, I take a deep breath and read three affirmations: "I manage my bills with ease," "My bills are paid off quickly and effortlessly," and "I choose abundance." I pause as I breathe and let these affirmations sink in. I smile because I believe in the power of affirmations! What was once stressful, is now simple. I have always read affirmation statements, but I used to rattle them off like I was reading a grocery list. Now when I read them, I slow down, I think about the meaning of the words, and I visualize my dreams and goals. These extra steps make my whole body tingle as I smile and feel the joy of the affirmation. This makes the statement real, possible and exciting. I certainly want to feel good while I pay bills because I know that my emotions are guiding me. The better I feel, the more effortless it becomes. This has made a tremendous difference in my financial life. Abundance has shown up in so many unexpected ways that I now have a deep faith that all is well.

Now that I understand how my emotions affect the events of my life, I have learned to harness positive energy—even in the worst of times—and that positive energy has given me the clarity to make better decisions. I now set clear intentions for my day and things don't happen to me haphazardly. I have much more control of my life experiences.

It took time, and I learned—slowly. I longed for relief, so I encouraged myself to trust the process. As negative thoughts popped up, I gently redirected them and focused on people or memories that made me feel warm and happy. If I started to stress about my son, I remembered his laughter or something fun we did together and instantly felt better. If I forgot to pay a bill, I gently told myself it wasn't the end of the world. I would think about all the bills that I did pay and how responsible and organized I am. That felt great. So as thoughts came up that made me anxious or angry, I would focus on something that made me feel good. One thought at a time.

As days and weeks went by, I would soothe myself with positive thoughts and images. If my mother made a sarcastic comment or a coworker dumped work on me, I would breathe through it and shake it off. Anger and depression seemed to be the first emotions that popped up, but I now had tools to turn them around. I would think about Emmet Fox's *The Golden Key to Prayer* and say, "God is guiding me now," because I vowed never to let anything or anyone ruin my entire day again. Initially, the relief from a situation would only last a few minutes. As time went on, I could get through longer stretches without being annoyed, exasperated, angry, or blue. I was relentless in my pursuit of positive thinking. If I started to wallow in self-pity, I reminded myself that if I wanted my life to look and feel great, I had to put out different thoughts. I wanted to manifest joy and a beautiful home, vacations, and financial freedom. If I kept holding on to my miseries, I was only going to get more of the burdens already on my plate. I wanted to clear the plate to allow the new to come in. I had to shake off all hard feelings I was lugging around and focus on what was good in my life and watch it grow. And *grow* it did.

Not only do I feel better now, but the process helped me become less judgmental and more patient and empathetic. It helped me become a more compassionate teacher and school supervisor, a more engaged wife, mother, daughter, and friend. As I gained deeper insights, I was much more available to people on a spiritual and emotional level.

Yet I still wasn't exactly where I wanted to be. I kept waiting for a level of vibrancy and zest I assumed would accompany my personal growth. At that time, I didn't appreciate how far I'd come, so I didn't have the ability to launch myself to the next level. I continued to persevere: I prayed, I meditated, I attended workshops, I read, and I journaled daily. I created a daily gratitude ritual and really began to appreciate all aspects of my life—even the ones that weren't perfect. With time, it all came together, and I have come to realize how deeply blessed I am. My confidence has soared as I consciously control my thoughts and decisions, so I can shape my life exactly the way I want it. Today, I am deeply grateful and consider myself a *very* lucky person. One of the main reasons I'm writing this book is to help people who may feel frustrated and stuck—like I once did—understand how to lead a brighter more fulfilling life.

This book is about the practical skills I have developed that have given me the clarity and confidence to even begin pursuing my goals or feel worthy enough to dream them in the first place. I have come to realize that a couple of things in my life were holding me back. First, my parents—and I love them dearly—didn't have the skills to teach me how to navigate the ups and downs of life. In my family, if you did something wrong, no one talked to you for weeks. If someone was upset, he/she would fall into bed in a dark room for days. "Woe is me," was definitely the theme in my house.

When you have grown up this way and it's all you see day in and day out for years, the patterns become imbedded into your personality without the realization that you're carrying them around. So every time something wasn't working out for me, I would immediately get sad, turn inward, and mope. I was comfortable with these emotions because I knew them well! I really didn't have any other coping skills.

I have a client who grew up in a house where everyone was angry at one another all the time. She immediately flips the angry switch when something isn't going her way. I have another client who is always frowning—just like her mother. She wasn't conscious of her facial expression or the fact that it was more of a learned behavior than her own natural tendency. Our reactions may just be deeply ingrained blueprints that we can change, but first we have to be aware of the patterns in our lives that show up over and over again. You need to know what you need to change.

I believe that these patterns hold us back from manifesting our desires. Now, when life's ups and downs show up and I feel myself getting deflated, I pause, breathe, and realize I can handle any problem that comes my way. I release the depression and crankiness that try to seep in. I've learned that if I focus on feeling depressed, I will only bring more depression into my life. So when I feel down, I think about something else. I love looking up at all the brilliant colors in the sky; it's hard to be depressed when nature is so vivid and spectacular. Sometimes I get a mint chocolate chip ice cream cone with chocolate sprinkles. That always lifts my mood—and for that moment, I don't focus on the calories! As I consistently practice lifting my mood, my mood seems pretty wonderful these days. I wake up content and my emotions and energy level are consistently positive all day long. Of course I have moments when things aren't so great, but I change my thoughts, so my day gets better quickly. Sometimes the evening can be tricky; it is very clear to me now that if I'm tired or hungry, I'm not in the best place to deal with difficult issues or circumstances. The best thing for me to do is ease down* and relax.

What I realize now is that people who are always smiling have great coping skills. They also have problems, but they know how to manage them. With all this new awareness, I am able to stay centered, understand my nature, embrace my strengths and weaknesses, and love myself. It isn't always easy and satisfaction isn't always instant, but I'm gentle and patient as I watch my growth and progress. Esther says you are not here to get it done; you are here for the journey. It's important that we embrace the processes of life.

Another valuable lesson that I have learned is that everyone is lucky. No one is purposely being punished while others are being rewarded. That was a huge relief. In Emmet Fox's *The Golden Key*, he writes, "God is omnipotent, and man is His image and likeness, and has dominion over all things. This is the inspired teaching, and it is intended to be taken literally, at its face value. Man means every man, and so the ability to draw on this power is not the special prerogative of the mystic or the saint, as is so often supposed, or even of the highly trained practitioner. Whoever you are, wherever you might be, the Golden Key to harmony is in your hands right now." We all deserve to have the life we want to live—to be happy, satisfied, comfortable, and confident.

In this book, I share with you the skills that have helped me get to a place where I believe that my life is wonderful, and I'm genuinely happy and grateful. I found ways to fill, nurture, and love myself, so I could feel worthy and ready to accept all the wonderful gifts life has to offer.

Asking, Believing, and Receiving are paramount for the Law of Attraction to work. For me to be in a place of believing that I could attract the life I wanted, I had to feel worthy. I knew I could ask for little things, but the big things that I dreamed of just didn't seem within my reach. For me to be in a place of receiving, I had to believe that I deserved the riches life has to offer. They weren't reserved for a group of elite people. I had access to them too! I had to allow good things to happen to me, and appreciate the daily miracles that I usually took for granted: when traffic opens up and I get to work on time, when my son pitches a perfect baseball game, when lucrative work opportunities just show up, and the list could go on and on. I am in the moment instead of longing for my future. I was missing all the sweet details of my life because I was waiting for a McMansion to fall on my front lawn. I now have a deep appreciation for my cozy cottage where I live with my husband, son, and our Bassett Hound. I appreciate everything with a deeper satisfaction, awareness, and awe.

As all these ideas have sorted themselves for me, my energy level has skyrocketed! I was always tired and drained because my energy was scattered everywhere. I was angry and anxious all the time. Now I protect my energy and use it in ways that serve me; I don't give it away anymore. You may be thinking, but how do you do that? It didn't happen instantaneously, and, as you read this book, the tips will help you focus and release all the things that aren't working in your life.

I have come to accept that I can't control other people's behaviors. I have released a lot of bottled up energy this way—whether at home, at work, or with friends and family. I try to listen more, and I also appreciate that everyone has their own way of living and thinking about life—even my young son! I can't make anyone else see my point of view. Everyone has a unique perspective that makes sense to that person. I can only take care of *my own* growth and make sure that *my* perspective is clear and that all *I* do is moving *me* in a direction where *I* want to go. And some days I have to remind myself to nurture my energy and use it to comfort my soul. I'm still working on this pattern. Maybe I always will be, but now I have enough awareness to remind myself—gently—that I can't take on other people's pain or responsibilities. I can only manage my own.

Another very important component of all this is that it takes time. Just like going on vacation requires you to plan the trip, book the reservations, pack, get to the airport, check in, go through security—all before you arrive at your beautiful destination—working on yourself takes time, and you are worth it! Even though I feel great about so many aspects of my life, I'm still a work in progress. I read this great advice over and over, so I feel joy as I appreciate my life. I love growing emotionally and spiritually. This is my path forever.

Each chapter contains eleven sensational, yet simple ideas in specific areas to help you believe that you can have the love, joy, and abundance you want. I chose the number 11 because it is a powerful number for manifesting! At the end of each chapter, I have included testimonials from my coaching clients. I think it's important for you to read about other people and how they use the tools I provide in this book to navigate the chaos in their lives. One of my goals in writing this book is to share that everyone is constantly struggling. If you live or work with people, you are constantly bombarded with situations that require your attention and action. I've learned that once you feel good about yourself, you will have energy to handle any situation in your life with grace and ease.

11

Get Happy to Attract the Life You Want!

"It's only a thought, and a thought can be changed"

Louise Hay, author

According to author Doreen Virtue, the number 11 reminds us to keep our thoughts positive because they are manifesting instantly into form! Focus only upon your desires and not your fears (angeltherapy.com). This introductory chapter, *Get Happy to Attract the Life You Want*, is the foundation we need to embrace as we move forward on our journey to feel great. Some of the ideas may seem repetitive and that's on purpose because feeling good is a practice. Bring this awareness into your day, so you know that all day long you are going to consciously focus on aspects of life that feel good. You are going to have some moments that are difficult, and that's when you have to be patient with yourself and consciously get back to practicing great feeling thoughts. If you are like me, and you spent many years in a negative place, this will also take perseverance. The negative thoughts are going to want to creep in, and you are going to have to be steadfast in clearing them away. I visually throw my negative thoughts deep into the center of the earth where the magma quickly burns them up. Sometimes I put my negative thoughts on a cloud and let them float away. This leaves room for the positive thoughts I'm attracting to have room to grow and take hold in my mind. Practice, patience and perseverance are necessary to achieve any long term happiness. As you read the eleven practices below, think about how you can apply them to your life in a meaningful, consistent way.

1. Our lives are supposed to feel good. When you wake up in the morning, begin your day by deliberately focusing your attention on thoughts that are uplifting. Smile; smiling naturally raises your mood! Before you go to bed at night, use the meditative, restorative energy of sleep to dream and visualize your ideal life. Think sweet thoughts. Ask God for clarity about whatever is troubling you. You will be amazed at what your subconscious can do for you while you sleep!

2. Feel joy; be happy—no matter what. Initially, you may think—just like I did—it is impossible. Build on your momentum* of happiness. Abraham talks about a 17 second momentum rule. If you think about something for 17 seconds, you are building momentum with that thought. So if you have a positive feeling thought and then another and then another...just writing that makes me smile! You want to grow what is positive in your life. Think

of it as the snowball effect. If something is going to grow into a giant snowball that is going to barrel down the steep slope of your life, make sure it's exactly what you want! It's a matter of training your mind to focus on what is working in your life. On my worst days, I enjoy the sun on my face. I always get pleasure out of looking at the clouds in the sky. If I get frustrated with my husband, I remember that he cooks dinner most nights, or I picture how cute it is to see him play baseball with our son. I can't stay angry, and I build positive momentum this way. The more you focus on the positive, the more it grows in your life. I will be conscious of my thoughts for the rest of my life because I feel so wonderful, confident and capable with my new attitude of gratitude. It isn't always easy, but life is a journey. We're allowed to have bad days, but don't stay in that dark, murky place. Listen to your favorite songs, read affirmations, look for positive quotes on your phone, or take a few deep breaths! Give yourself the gift of a few minutes to focus on something pleasant, and you'll feel the joy permeate your body!

3. Decide what you want to do, be, and have. In Jack Canfield's book, *The Success Principles*, he recommends an exercise where you create a list of the 30 things you want to do, the 30 things you want to have, and the 30 things you want to be before you die. Be clear about what you want. When my friend's father died, she asked him to send her a man. She was hoping for a husband. Instead, her sister had three sons. She didn't specify the type of relationship she clearly wanted, so she got her man in three nephews!

4. Find time to daydream and visualize your goals and ideal life. Spiritual/motivational authors talk about vision boards all the time. Check out John Assaraf's *The Complete Vision Board Kit*, or read Shakti Gawain's *Creative Visualization*, so you can

have a deeper understanding of the power of visualization. Take the time to make one, or at least picture your dreams vividly in your mind. When I do this, I can't help but smile. It relaxes me and brings me to a wonderful place where I believe my dreams can come true! Remember to always put yourself in the visual of what you want or you could be manifesting it for someone else!

5. Everyone experiences problems—the difference between someone who feels like a victim and someone who feels like a victor is the victor has coping skills, including a positive mental attitude, which enables him/her to work through and find solutions. A victor understands that problems are part of life and moves forward to find a solution that builds his/her confidence. When a problem arises, instead of thinking, "Why me?" A victor says, "Okay, how do I resolve this? What is the solution?"

A victim fights/resists a problem; a victim will stew, blame, and tell everybody about it, which feeds the problem and builds negative momentum. Remember, when you build negative momentum, a problem can feel like a giant snowball barreling down the slope of a steep hill. Once a problem gains that much power, it feels like an insurmountable monster in your mind. You want to stop negative momentum before it gains any power or speed! Always stay in the solution.

Stop worrying. It drains your energy and doesn't change anything. Focus on the solution and move forward.

6. Know your triggers: certain people, alcohol, food, family events, or holidays trigger us to behave in ways that are counterproductive. I can't go into a pub and not eat a cheeseburger. When I'm tired and hungry, it's not the time to call my son's teacher or look at his grades online. It's not the time

to discuss finances with my husband. I've learned that it's okay to give myself a break to avoid barreling into lose-lose situations head on. I give myself permission to rest or read a book. I know in the morning when I'm refreshed and all my buttons are reset, I can manage anything. Understand your mood and choose your battles.

7. Practice patience with yourself and others. We want things done NOW! We force things or bulldoze our way in the name of what we think is right. Breathe. If something is not working out, ease down before you jump in and try to "fix it." You may want to go to Belize on a vacation, but your partner is excited about hiking the Appalachian Trail. Your child may want to play soccer, but you had your heart set on him/her playing lacrosse. Before you dig your heels in and demand things are done your way, take a step back—try to watch the events in your life like a movie or a tube floating down a lazy river. It's

amazing how much perspective you gain when you stop treating life like everything is an emergency or there's only one fixed way to do things—*Your Way*. Open up to letting things unfold organically. When we force things and stifle people, we feel like we've won, but at what cost? If everyone around you is miserable and tense, take a close look at that. The good news is, when you relax and start to trust the process, everyone wins!

8. Feel gratitude. Wake up and think grateful thoughts. Be happy for the warm, comfortable bed you just slept in. Be happy that you can open your eyes and see. Be happy you can get out of bed and jump into a hot shower. Do you get my drift? We take so much for granted in our lives. It's beautiful to pause and appreciate the awesomeness that we can see, hear, touch, taste, and feel. Life gives us an abundance of gifts. Throughout the day, take the time to pause and smile about something that

brings you joy. Abraham says this shifts or pivots your energy in the direction of your desires.

9. Allow yourself to feel the joy. Allow yourself to accept the gifts that life has to offer. It's not enough to understand the Law of Attraction on an intellectual level. You have to feel it. When you accept gifts or compliments from others, when you appreciate everything about your life (the ups *and* the downs), when you feel joy, you will have ***achieved allowing***. We all know how to ask for something, but we don't always allow or receive well. Sometimes you'll say you want something, but your immediate reaction is, "I can't afford it." You've just cut yourself off from Allowing. Ask and then breathe, and allow yourself to feel that you've already received your manifestation. In our society, we praise the active, busy, fiercely independent part of ourselves; however, that can be counterproductive because it disconnects

us from accepting and receiving. The contentment comes from experiencing all three: wanting, allowing, and receiving. The best way to be in a state of allowing is to meditate, listen, observe, watch, feel grateful, and appreciate—these are the receptive states that our society usually deems passive. But it is in the passivity and relaxed state where clarity comes.

10. When you realize that everything you think, say, and do has created the results in your life so far, you will deliberately and intentionally think, say, and do only what aligns with your purpose and goals. If you treat your words like they are magic, you will be careful with what you say. Do you really want to put it out to the universe that: "I have no luck" or "I never have enough money" or "I can never catch a break." My girlfriend always says, "It's hard" about everything in her life—whether it's her son going on a job interview or her commute to work. Guess what? Her life *is* hard! When

you understand the Law of Attraction, you will choose words, thoughts and actions that support a wonderful life.

11. It takes time to shape your life so it feels brilliant. It will eventually feel effortless, but initially, it may feel uncomfortable. Be easy and gentle with yourself. As you continually refrain from old patterns and focus your attention and intention on what you truly want, you are going to feel great. Your confidence will soar. I feel this deep satisfaction knowing that everything is working out for me.

Testimonials:

Before I met Georgette, I didn't realize how angry I was and how it was affecting my family. I keep her book in my bag and nightstand to remind me to focus on the positive. I'm committed to retraining my brain, especially since my family has noticed. My son told me that Thanksgiving dinner was actually pleasant because I wasn't barking. Through my coaching with Georgette, I'm releasing my need to be perfect. I let people bring food and I delegated responsibilities throughout the day. It was the first holiday where I wasn't exhausted and angry. My family was so happy! Georgette has helped me see and believe that I can make simple changes that have brought me and my family joy and peace. —Maria

I have utilized the teachings in Georgette's book to help me through some difficult obstacles in my life. The book has become a guide that clears pathways so I can walk through my life easier and maintain my footing no matter what the negativity I am dealing with. If you are looking for a book to help you see light where there may only appear to be darkness in your life, I highly suggest reading this and using it as a key to carrying you when times are hard. —Patrick

11

Brilliant Dating

"I never loved another person the way I loved myself."

Mae West, actress

These ideas are based in your best interest. They may seem old-fashioned and virtuous, but they are paramount when your self-worth is your priority. We don't like to feel that someone is taking advantage of us or using us. By following these practices and ideas, you are taking care of yourself, which will naturally boost your confidence, which will naturally lead to your making better decisions about who you date and love.

1. When we meet or like someone, we spend so much time hoping he/she likes us—we forget to ask ourselves, "Do *I* really like this person?" It's so sad that we look for external validation from strangers instead of *knowing* how wonderful we are. It's so important that we build our internal confidence, and we do this through loving ourselves first. When you love yourself completely and step into that power, your feelings won't be hurt if someone isn't attracted to you. You will understand that when the right person comes along, it will all come together naturally and perfectly. You won't have to stress or worry about it.

2. We bend over backwards to please someone, but we never stop to ask ourselves, "What does this person do for me?" When my gorgeous girlfriend met a guy who lived an hour away, she drove to his house every weekend. He never took the road trip to her place. Another beautiful girlfriend just met someone and their relationship

consists of her cooking him dinner all the time. All he has to do is show up. Again, we are looking for external validation of our worth. When we feel good about ourselves, we are centered and don't need to prove ourselves to anybody. Then it will be a natural expectation that the relationship has balance.

3. Be clear about what you want in a relationship. Don't focus on what you don't want. Make a declaration such as, "I want someone who cares about me and nurtures me. I want to be with someone who supports me emotionally, spiritually, physically, and financially." These affirmations are much more powerful and effective than, "I don't want another loser."

4. Set boundaries with electronics. You may think someone cares about you because he/she's texting all day, but that's not the case. We end up staring at the phone all day pining for the "ting" of a text message. Turn the phone off at work and check it

at lunch. If you're having dinner with a friend, colleague or business associate, turn it off. If you're going out for drinks with friends, turn it off. It will be difficult, but again, as you set a boundary, you're putting yourself in control. You are no longer some wayward child falling apart if the phone doesn't "ting" every five minutes. You're giving someone—who isn't even in the room—all the power. Build your confidence and your brilliance by turning off the phone and putting it away. I highly recommend you do this at night before you go to sleep as well. I promise it's the best feeling in the world.

5. When you're dating, it doesn't mean you're "saving" someone. A relationship is supposed to be mutually satisfying. If someone asks you to borrow money, *RUN!* We confuse red flags with wanting to rescue someone—like the person is a puppy! Women love to feel needed. When I see gorgeous, brilliant, talented,

successful women in Hollywood throw themselves at men, it scares me to think how prevalent this practice is! We think it means love, but we quickly resent it when our needs aren't being met. If someone is incapable of fulfilling your needs, it doesn't make him/her a bad person. He/She is just not the right person for you. Again, we want to meet someone who enhances us, who makes us feel good, and who has the capacity to care about us deeply.

6. Don't have sex until you're sure you want to be in a relationship with someone. Abstinence is difficult, but powerful. It allows you to be so clear about who the person is before you get emotionally attached. Once you sleep with someone, you get entwined. That makes it difficult to move on if the person isn't right for you. You gain so much confidence from being in control of your sex life.

7. Don't drink on the first few dates. Treat them like a job interview. Would you

drink before an interview? Of course not! You want to be sharp and on your game. Why would you be anything less when you're getting to know someone who could possibly be your mate for life?

8. Don't talk about your ex-boyfriends/ex-girlfriends. You've just met someone new—treat it like a fresh start. Show that person your positive vibrant self. Smile and have fun!

9. Don't take every date seriously. If you're dating online, just meet people for coffee or a walk. Have fun and practice the art of dating! Practice the art of conversation! Just don't go on a date when you're feeling lonely and vulnerable. It's a recipe for disaster. Avoid lose-lose situations.

10. There are millions of people out there—you will meet someone. You only need to meet one nice person! Have faith. The more you believe, the faster it will happen.

11. Don't fret if you aren't meeting the type of person you want. My client feels that she's always attracting losers. Not true. There are many different types of people in the world. Many different people will be attracted to you—you don't have to date them. Be choosy and wait for the right person to come along. Be firm and don't waste time with someone who doesn't fulfill your needs. Only you have the control and patience to weed through potential suitors to find the right person who makes you happy!

Testimonials:

Georgette's advice is liberating! I used to meet a girl and immediately make long term plans because I so anxiously wanted a deep relationship. After a disastrous divorce, I sought Georgette's help. She helped me understand that I needed a new skill set, so I wouldn't repeat my mistakes. It took a while, but I am happy to say, I feel great. I dated a lot, but saw the red flags quickly and moved away from the relationships. I have met a wonderful woman, but I am moving slowly. She recently asked me to meet her parents. We'd have to drive two hours and stay at their house. In the past, I would've said yes even though I knew it would be a disaster. This time I said, "No thanks. I have a lot going on this weekend." She said, "Okay." There was no arguing. It was so simple. I can't believe I'm 50 and just learning how to date! Thank you, Georgette. —Sean

Georgette has taught me how to listen. I dated someone for three years who was clear that he didn't want a commitment. I didn't believe him. I kept waiting for him to change, but he kept telling me that he wasn't interested in a serious relationship. I was frustrated and angry. Georgette taught me that it wasn't his fault! He was being honest with me and I was refusing to accept the truth. With Georgette's help, I got very clear on what I was looking for in a relationship. I wanted a loving, supporting partner. She helped me set my standards high. I ended the relationship and spent some time working on myself. I am happy to say I am now in a great relationship with a wonderful man who loves me! —Jennifer

11

Brilliant Marriage

"If we are peaceful, if we are happy, we can smile, and everyone in our family, our entire society, will benefit from our peace."

Thich Nhat Hanh, Vietnamese Monk

The beginning of most relationships is euphoric, but most of us don't know how to work through challenging times. Many people believe that when you start disagreeing, it signals the end of the union. It isn't easy for any two people—even when they love each other—who have different backgrounds and expectations to come together and see eye-to-eye on issues involving daily living. Then let's throw into the mix that most people don't have great communication skills to articulate their needs, so they feel disappointed, overwhelmed, or unhappy with the relationship. If you can overcome difficult times with your partner, the relationship blossoms in ways you didn't know were possible. Below are some thoughts, skills and tools to navigate the stresses in a meaningful way. (Please note that I'm not advocating for staying in a relationship or marriage that is emotionally, physically, spiritually, or financially abusive or destructive.)

1. We enter marriage naively. I don't know why dating is a prerequisite for marriage. Everyone is dressed up and on their best behavior! We have to be patient, loving, kind and supportive if a relationship is going to thrive in a harmonious way. Marriage has a lot of growing pains. People expect the ideal image portrayed in movies and books. Marriage can be like still water, it can be like a wild canoe trip on the Colorado River, and you have to be ready for both. Some issues last years, some last minutes, but the beauty comes when two

people are committed to each other. One of my favorite suggestions is to think about what happens when you are arguing with your spouse; you are taking opposing sides. That puts a wedge between you, which only weakens the relationship. Come together as a team because a team works to win. Put aside your differences and ask the question, "How can we compromise so we are both satisfied with a solution?" Now you are working together, which will only strengthen your relationship.

2. When I need to have a difficult conversation with my husband, I prepare. I find that if I can remain in neutral, which include my facial expressions, body language, and tone of voice, I have a better chance of articulating what I need to say without making him defensive. If my goal is to get him to understand what I need, it is best if I can express it without judgment or blaming. If I can stay in the facts without rolling my eyes or raising my voice, we

can usually get through a conversation and come up with a mutually satisfying solution.

3. In my most difficult moments, I am always grateful for my family. I am grateful for the companionship, the comfort, the closeness, and the strength I get from them. I may be tired and overwhelmed by the pile of laundry and dishes in the sink, but I wouldn't want my life to look any other way. When my husband and I have financial struggles or we don't see eye-to-eye on important issues, I am grateful first, and then I focus on solving the situation with him.

4. There are always two sides to a story. No matter what I'm feeling, I try to understand my partner's point of view. I'm not perfect, I'm not always right, and I'm not always easy. I try to shelf my stubbornness and be open to listening and learning.

5. You can't change anyone—only yourself. I have seen so many unhappy couples

stubbornly try to get their spouse to behave a certain way, only to find their efforts useless. Some couples fight over the same thing for years (I wish you were more social, I wish you were excited to decorate the house, Why can't you be nice to my friends, etc.). All it does is wear away at the relationship. Don't waste your energy wishing your partner would act a certain way or do certain things. Focus all your energy on being your best-self. Sometimes when you leave someone alone, and the person sees you enjoying your life, he/she comes around, but don't bank on that. Focus on being your happiest self. I have friends who I meet for dinner regularly. If I need my house painted, I don't wait for my husband to do it. I hire someone. I don't want to tear our relationship apart over things that have simple solutions. There are ways to compromise, so you can both be satisfied.

6. When I heard about the fourth step in Alcoholics Anonymous, I was blown

away. "What's your part in it? List all people, places, things, institutions, ideas or principles with which you are angry with, resentful of, feel hurt or threatened by. Here we list our part in the resentment; we list where we were at fault. What's the truth here? Where was my responsibility in this resentment, what part do I own? What might I have done differently?"

In the past, when I was angry at my husband, I never thought I had a part in it! But now I know better. Am I really surprised by my husband's behaviors? Didn't I know him well before we got married? Most people naively think their partner is going to change after marriage or somewhere in the longevity of the relationship. We are fooling ourselves. Yes, of course people can change, but if you marry someone expecting different behaviors, you may be disappointed. My friend married someone who used cocaine and she knew his addiction was extreme. She's very angry

that he's a drug addict, but the behavior was there before they got married! There were red flags everywhere flashing, "Danger!" She chose to walk down the aisle with this man and has to take responsibility for that. That's the hard part because it's so much easier to blame the other person. Once we own our decisions, then we can move forward and find solutions.

7. Consideration, Compromise, and Compassion—especially in those moments when these are the last qualities you want to exhibit! You and your partner are two people in a dance—it's a constant give and take. The more we can respect each other, the more likely we can resolve issues and build a strong, healthy relationship.

8. Don't do anything that makes you feel resentful. If you're angry it doesn't serve anyone. For a while, my husband would ask me to bring him lunch to work. It was cute, and I enjoyed our time together.

After a while, I started to resent it. I was tired from running around with our son, working, errands, etc. One day while I was driving, I was really angry. That's when I realized I had a choice. I could say no. I didn't whine, complain or act like a martyr. Because I was able to state the facts, my husband understood, and it didn't become an argument.

9. It's okay to have separate lives. You don't always have to do everything together. We fell in love with someone because of who he/she was in the moment. When we demand that our significant others stop playing music, golf, volleyball or whatever other hobbies, activities, or friends they had when we met them, we are chipping away at their personality. After a while, nothing is left—the person is a shadow of a former self. First, don't let anyone do this to you. Secondly, before you demand that someone change so drastically, realize that your loved one's best qualities may

disappear as his/her personality withers. Everyone loses.

10. It's all about perspective—we all grow up with our cultural norms and we believe what we have been taught is right. It's the only way. For example, women cook dinner. Men take out the garbage. The man has to be the breadwinner. There are so many different roles we can take as a couple if we are willing to be open and flexible. I have been able to release a lot of anger and resentment by allowing our relationship to grow. I believe the reason I was able to write this book is because I released a lot of societal pressure to have my marriage and our roles in the marriage look a certain way. Don't try to control everything and force it to be "Your Way." It's a recipe for misery.

11. When we are in a relationship, we have to make a choice about whether we want to be happy. Are you always looking for

things wrong in your relationship? Do you spend enough time thinking about what is right about the relationship? Sometimes we aren't even cognizant that we bring so much of our own baggage into our relationships. Sometimes we even bring our parents' baggage. Take the time to think about, analyze, and reflect on your perceptions and behaviors. Some people damage their relationship by complaining about their spouse all the time. Are you sabotaging your relationship? If you are, make small changes daily to bring joy into your relationship. That should be our ultimate goal—to create beautiful memories for our family.

Testimonials:

Georgette has taught me to stop and take a breath before I talk to my wife about difficult topics. In the past, I used to get angry and frustrated and say whatever I was thinking, which was not always constructive. It always ended in a big fight, and we wouldn't talk for days. By pausing and thinking before I say something and trying different approaches that don't make her feel defensive, we now have deep conversations. Our marriage has never been better! —Rudy

I didn't realize that I brought so much baggage into my marriage. My parents fought all the time so I automatically respond to everything with negativity. With Georgette's help, I am changing my attitude and focusing on the positive. My husband and I enjoy hiking, spending weekends away, and eating in the city with friends. We are focusing on doing a lot more of what makes us happy. Now when we have a problem, we deal with it swiftly and work to compromise because we are focused on being happy. —Stacy

11

Brilliant Personal Relationships

"You can't always choose your coworkers or family members, but you can make better choices about how you feel every moment of every day."

Georgette Van Vliet, author

We all have difficult people in our lives, and for me, being able to manage these relationships with grace and dignity is key. Once you develop practices to help you navigate difficult situations, you won't be so emotionally charged. I don't even remember what used to bother me because I am so focused on my own well-being.

1. One of my favorite tips is to practice staying in neutral. Neutral means your facial expressions aren't negative (you aren't

rolling your eyes, frowning, making beady eyes), your body language isn't screaming anger (hands on hip, arms across the chest, shoulders tense), and your tone of voice is calm (no sarcasm, raising your voice, etc.). You might want to practice neutral in the mirror before you talk to someone about something that is bothering you. The other key to having a conversation in neutral is that you speak in facts. The minute you say something that is accusatory, blaming, or judgmental, the conversation usually deteriorates. When you speak in neutral, a wonderful thing happens. The person will listen to you without feeling defensive. You will be able to focus on the topic at hand without anyone feeling offended.

2. Learn how to say, "No thank you." When people impose on us by asking us to do things such as babysit or help them move, we feel guilty saying no, but inside we are miserable! I highly recommend that you learn to say, "No thank you."

It's a simple statement. You don't have to explain yourself further. People will learn to respect you when you can communicate without apologizing. Stay neutral and say, "No thank you," simply and clearly. Don't worry—people will find others to help them.

3. Don't focus on the negative, which builds negative momentum. I have coworkers that bicker all the time. Recently they were fighting over a file cabinet! This is what happens when you are so angry with someone that even a file cabinet will get under your skin. Of course, this applies to all our relationships. If you've been with your partner for a long time, resentments can seep in. Don't let them. Try to release anything that weakens the relationship and try to build all that is good. I'm not saying that you shouldn't deal with problems, but when you are in neutral you can talk about them in a way that isn't critical, judgmental, blaming, or accusatory. All these negative

descriptors only cause people to feel defensive, which will start an argument. Your goal is to open a conversation and you have a better chance of being heard when you are in neutral.

Analyze if your childhood patterns have created negative momentum in you. My parents were always fighting, and even after they divorced, they bickered constantly for the past 30 years. It didn't stop until my dad died last year. Is it any wonder that I brood and don't always feel satisfied with my personal relationships? With this in mind, when I get annoyed and irritated, I breathe through it and reflect, "Is this real or is this just the negativity that I project?" 99% of the time it's the negativity I project. I use this practice with my friends, coworkers, my spouse, my son, and other people in my life. I have been able to chip away at a lot of negativity with this awareness.

4. Don't argue with difficult people - they love confrontations! You're feeding them.

You want to cut the energy supply and let them fade away.

5. Deflate people. Sometimes when we get upset with someone, we talk about it endlessly, which only magnifies the negative feelings. I love to close my eyes and visualize the person as a paperclip—tiny with no power over me. Sometimes I imagine the person like an inflatable bouncy house and I get to pull the plug, so all the air is taken out and the person collapses on the floor, just like the bouncy house would. Sometimes I have to practice this visual several times over a period of days and weeks, but eventually, the situation doesn't have the same grip on me. I'm able to release a lot by doing this.

6. Cut the cord. If I'm having a hard time with someone, I visualize that there is a cord connecting us. Sometimes the cord is like a thin rope and other times it is as thick as the steel that holds up the George

Washington Bridge. I visualize cutting the cord that keeps us energetically together. It helps release some of the tension, and when I feel the connection with the other person lessen, I can deal with it better. Sometimes if the negative feelings are really strong, I have to cut the cord several times throughout the day or over a week. But eventually it does make it easier. It won't have so much of a hold on me.

7. What if toxic people were put on this earth to jar and shock us so we don't remain complacent? What if their actions and behaviors force us to move to another town or get another job? What if it's our destiny and we should be grateful to the toxic people for giving us the shove we need? This is the best advice I got from Oprah Winfrey's "The Whispers." Whenever someone is acting toxic around me, it makes me think, "Is there a lesson for me here? Is there something I'm supposed to do differently and this is my clue?" This

has helped me so many times in my life. Now I believe life should look like a walk on the Red Carpet. Life should flow that smoothly. When things aren't going well and I'm frustrated or angry over a period of time with no solution in sight, I look at my options and consider that my life is supposed to move in a different direction.

8. Get a thicker skin. There is a situation in my life that used to show up a lot and it really irritated me. I always felt left out. I felt like people at work were doing things together; people in my community held events, and I was never included. Whenever I would see a group of them together, it made me angry. Then one day I decided I needed a thicker skin; I knew I had to stop letting everything irritate me if I wanted to feel joy in my life. I looked these situations in the eye and forced myself to be tougher. It has worked. It's amazing how these situations don't have any power over me anymore. It's a great lesson because the negative feelings

faded away once I didn't give them any attention.

9. Be an observer before you react. A few years ago, I had a recurring situation at work with some coworkers that was very uncomfortable. I decided to just watch the interactions like I was watching a movie. I didn't say anything. I didn't judge it. I didn't get emotional about it. I just kept telling myself, "I'm gathering information." This kept me in neutral for an entire week! When the week ended, the most beautiful thing happened. Something that had annoyed me to pieces no longer had a grip on me. It was incredibly liberating to realize that I didn't have to do anything and the solution came naturally.

10. Stop banging your head against the wall trying to get people to like you. The rejection and disrespect are horrible for your self-esteem. I used to give people rides to airports and waste two hours driving

when I would rather be doing something fun! I even drove someone across the country once. I was so angry and resentful, and the person wasn't even grateful. Make yourself the most important person in your life! When you focus on the people who bring you joy, happiness will permeate your being.

Be aware if you have a high tolerance for intolerable behavior. Do your friends always cancel plans at the last minute? Does your boyfriend disappear a lot just to show up a few days later with lame excuses? Is your girlfriend impatient with you and then blames her mood swings on PMS? Does your mother-in-law expect you to drop everything and cook her dinner or drive her somewhere? This list could go on and on, and sometimes when we don't feel good about ourselves, we are vulnerable to people's excuses. Yes, sometimes things happen, but if you see a pattern of neglect, address it with the person. Move away from situations that hurt your self-esteem. If something isn't feeling good, reflect on what is best for you and then do what is best to protect yourself.

We teach people how to treat us. You have to learn to love yourself first before you can love someone else. When you love yourself, it will be easy to set boundaries with people. Now that I feel great, I will never let someone abuse me. I very clearly say, "No thank you" to anything that doesn't serve me. You won't let people mistreat you because it doesn't feel good.

11. Don't split the energy. So many of us love our family and friends, but complain all the time about annoying qualities they may have. Try to maintain positive momentum in your relationships. I complain that my mother drives me crazy, but in reality, she does everything for my family. That's what I should be talking about when my friends ask me how my mom is doing. Same thing

goes for my husband and best friend. I complain to my husband about my best friend, and I complain to my best friend about my husband! Now that I'm aware of how I split energy, I focus on keeping my word sacred. I say it all day long, "My word is sacred," because I am retraining myself to think about and nurture the connections I have with the people I care about most. I only say things that support the beauty I want to build in my life. I find that as I do this, my relationships are calmer, more loving, and connected.

Testimonials:

I didn't realize how much my depression and negative energy was affecting my relationships. Now when I feel down, I ask myself, "Is this real or is this a learned pattern that I'm carrying around?" Just asking the question seems to ease the negativity. Then I get up and move. I go to the gym, I go to a movie, I just keep moving because I realize that movement releases a lot of stuck energy. I definitely see more positivity in my life and my relationships thanks to Georgette's book. —Peter

Georgette has taught me that the things that annoy me are just triggers. Now I deal with situations that are difficult with grace and ease. I won't drink at family parties. I won't sit next to my sister-in-law at a barbecue. I don't do it in a mean way. In the past, I would pout and sit with my arms crossed over my chest because I was unhappy. It was obvious to everyone that I was in a bad mood. Georgette has taught me how to be neutral. I focus on the people who I want to talk to. She taught me to sidestep all the confrontations I've been having for the past 20 years with the same family members! I feel so free! I don't have anxiety thinking about events because I have great tools so I can deal with the people who make me crazy. One of my favorite tips is how to deflate an antagonist. Now I know how to sit back, relax and even enjoy myself. All thanks to Georgette's simple yet brilliant ideas! —Helene

11

Brilliant Self-Care

"As you ask for guidance, you are guided.
As you ask for wisdom, you are made wise."

Julia Cameron, author

1. Step out of your comfort zone more often, whether it means a new exercise class, traveling somewhere alone, or learning a new hobby. I met my husband when I joined an adult volleyball league at a local high school. Be open to doing things a new way. Even if it feels uncomfortable and surreal, push yourself through and stay on course. If your life isn't working the way you'd like it to, consider making changes.

You can't expect to continue the same behaviors but get different results.

2. We are powerful when we are rested, personally fulfilled, and consciously making the time to meet our needs. We won't get a Medal of Honor for neglecting ourselves. If you're running around because you think you are doing the right thing for your family or job, but you are miserable and exhausted, you might want to make some changes. Everyone around you will be happier if you are happier.

3. Meditate or find time to quiet your mind. The tranquility will center you and sometimes my most brilliant ideas come from silence. I gain a lot of clarity from taking a daily meditative walk. I also try to rest every day for at least 20 minutes.

4. Slow down for inspiration. We associate drive and power with effectiveness and success. I even see it at Disney World where parents drag their kids out of bed at 6am,

so they can get to every single attraction in the park. We live in a frenzy! It takes a lot of effort on my part to slow down, but it is necessary so I can have a clear focus on how to meet my goals. All spiritual authors advocate meditating, visualizing, taking the time to create goals and read them every day, journaling, and writing gratitude lists. The one thing all these actions have in common is that you have to stop, make time, and be conscious about what you are doing.

5. Nurture yourself. Most women associate nurturing with being selfish. That has such a negative connotation to it. The most important thing we can do is love and honor our soul and the precious skin that houses us. Practice extreme self-care. Find ways to honor your body. For me, it's acupuncture, massages, walking, and yoga. There are so many ways to get what you need when you become determined to take great care of yourself. I don't know why we

wear our exhaustion as a Badge of Honor. I am guilty of this, so every day I have to be conscious to do things that nurture me, especially eating well and exercising. Slow down and be gentle with yourself.

6. Don't let situations, relatives, friends, or partners zap your energy. We think we are being kind, caring and loving when we pour ourselves into someone, but sometimes the other person didn't even ask for our generosity. One of my clients went food shopping and filled her new boyfriend's fridge with enough food to last a week because he was running a marathon, and she wanted to make sure he felt supported. When he didn't thank her or even notice, she was furious! She didn't marry this man—I don't think they even ended up in a serious relationship. She meant well, but she could've used her time and energy to do something fulfilling for herself. Another client was dating someone and she did all the legwork to get his business registered

and off the ground. Again, she didn't marry this person, but she did an awful lot of running around and stressful, detail-oriented work for someone that probably didn't even appreciate the time and energy she gave. We have a tendency to give our time and energy away and save nothing for ourselves. Do we wonder why we feel depleted and exhausted? I've always joked that if I had the energy and time I've given away chasing relationships, I could earn a PhD! When we clean up our energy leaks, we feel revitalized and refreshed.

7. The rules for dating also apply to our family, friends and coworkers. If people are treating you badly or they make you uncomfortable, it's time to reflect on whether these relationships support your self-esteem and personal growth. The people closest to us should be our best cheerleaders and support system by building our confidence and self-worth. If you take inventory and you find this isn't

the case, you have decisions to make. I heard someone speak about this once, and he gave the best advice. He said he just distanced himself from some family members and business partners when he realized the relationships were toxic. He's not angry; there's no judgment; he just decided to quietly move on. What a concept! No yelling or screaming, "You're mean to me!" or, "Stop being a jerk!" This was liberating. I didn't have to hate someone. I didn't need a really bad scene as an excuse to move away from people who always had sharp and condescending comments to throw my way like daggers. As I did this, the most wonderful thing happened. One day while I was out to dinner with great friends, I realized that because I gently stepped away from negative people, I now have these new friends who are supportive and caring. And I have a lot of them! Always value your self-worth, your time and energy.

8. Before we feel depleted, we need to fill ourselves with whatever will bring us joy

and satisfaction. Do you want to visit at art gallery? Make time to do it. Do you want to see a Broadway Play? Make the arrangements. Do you want to visit Paris? Start planning the trip, even if it takes years to execute. I love to spend a weekend in the Hamptons in the spring before the crowds come. It's the most beautiful place on earth and never fails to satisfy me. Julia Cameron in her book, *The Artist's Way*, suggests an Artist's Date once a week where you do something fun, creative, spontaneous, and nurturing. It doesn't have to be expensive, and it's a way of receiving and opening yourself up to insight, inspiration, and guidance. It is a couple of hours that you guard and keep only for you. You take a walk around a city or new neighborhood, go see a movie, or meander through a second-hand store or a boutique. It is really about honoring the time commitment to yourself.

9. In another one of her books, *Finding Water*, Julia Cameron suggests setting

aside time weekly to walk. This isn't for physical exercise, but a time to put life into perspective. It's like a sorting process. When you set aside time for a solo walk in nature, your intuition and insight kick in. When you walk in nature, solutions to problems seem so clear. I love walking outside because it literally grounds me and makes me step out of myself. I look at the flowers, the sky, I look for deer—I'm not so focused on myself. It's a wonderful way to clear negativity and allow wisdom and clarity to lead the way.

10. Learn to say no when the people you love ask you to do something, but in your heart you know it's not in your best interest. Don't overextend yourself. My friend works long hours, and her job is stressful. One Sunday she was so exhausted, but promised her friend she'd meet her at the mall. She almost had an accident on the way home because she was so tired. It's so important that we protect ourselves, like a mother protects her little child.

11. Learn to say yes when an idea sparks a flame within you, it sounds exciting and you feel inspired to do it! If it makes you smile, say yes!

Testimonials:

Georgette's teachings have showed me that I can enjoy life. I work full-time and take care of my elderly mother, so I didn't get to go out much. I was angry about it all the time. I talked to Georgette after a seminar, and I was telling her my frustrations when she asked me to just look at the possibilities and solutions. Until then, I didn't think that there were any possibilities. But Georgette kept asking questions, and I realized that there were people who could help me with my mom. Now I go to movies and museums, and I even went to Europe. My mom is just fine! It's a miracle for me to know that when you put your mind to the solution, you can find ways to be happy. —Sharon

I am always depleted and exhausted. I feel like I have to be superwoman for my family. Georgette taught me that it's okay for me to enjoy my life. I go out to dinner with friends, and I don't feel guilty. I joined a book club, which is something I've wanted to do for years. The best part is that my family is happy for me! They encourage me to go out and have fun. I'm so happy! —Madeleine

11

Brilliant Body

"If we are to have magical bodies, we must have magical minds!"

Dr. Wayne Dyer, author

I won't say weight loss or diet anymore. I want to love my body! I want to look in the mirror and smile! I want to tuck my shirt into my jeans and wear a sterling silver, diamond studded belt buckle! I want that body confidence, and I deserve it. I will only put delicious, nutritious food in my body. I will exercise and feel strong. I will drink water all day long, so my skin radiates. I love everything about myself! Now that's a positive way to view your body!

1. Instead of focusing on what you can't eat, put a list of great, wholesome foods on your fridge that are perfect for you. Soup nurtures my soul. Hot tea also satisfies me and keeps me from overeating. Every week, I eat something new and different. I'm making adjustments that I can live with permanently.

2. Keep it simple. Limit: red meat, alcohol, soda, salt, sugar, carbs. Carbs convert to sugar, which converts to fat. No thank you! I'll choose healthier options that make me feel great.

3. Socialize in nature. My friends and I are always eating out, but those foods are loaded with salt and butter. I ask my friends to meet me for tea or a walk, so I curb all those take-out meals.

4. I focus on relaxation. I meditate and consciously practice the art of breathing, releasing tension from my shoulders and

letting go of all the daily pressure that builds up in my neck and chest. A lot of my overeating is stress eating. I drink more water, so I'm not throwing snacks down my throat. Relaxing and letting go are allowing me to make better food choices, find time to prepare quality meals, and to consciously put food to my lips. Taste it, acknowledge the flavor, chew it thoroughly, and then swallow. It is so important that we are present to what we are eating.

5. I smile when I look in the mirror. I like me. If you're hard on yourself, lighten up! I have great legs, so I accentuate them. Focus on your body parts that Rock!

6. Eat with a lobster fork or chopsticks. Someone told me that I eat too fast and that's why I gained weight. I watched her eat green beans, one bean at a time. She put the bean in her mouth and then put the fork down, chewed it thoroughly, and then put her fork in the next bean. She's

patient and eats slowly. I'm still working on this one. Don't forget to breathe in between bites!

7. Don't go to restaurants or places that trigger poor eating choices. There's a gourmet market by my job that serves fabulous salads. The problem is that they also serve smoked pastrami. There's no way I'm going to order a salad when I smell hot pastrami!

8. CARBS are EVERYWHERE! Don't be naive. I was making pastina for dinner thinking it was simple, warm and, I assumed, dietary. That was until I read the label and one ounce of pastina has 20 grams of carbs! These types of processed carbs don't support weight loss. I used to rush through the grocery store and throw boxes of protein bars and "low fat" food in my cart, but wonder why I can't lose belly fat. Now I read labels, and I'm shocked! Some of my most "precious" diet foods contain massive amounts of carbs. I now

focus on whole foods I enjoy that support the body I love.

9. Make time to cook and enjoy your creativity. Thich Nhat Hanh says preparing food is an art: be aware as you prepare to touch and feel the food. Find high quality markets that carry fresh organic foods. People complain about the cost but have no problem dropping $5 on a latte or $50 on fat-laden take-out. Awesome recipes are at our fingertips. Our priorities have to shift, so we are healthy and eat for vitality and well-being. Visualize the food you eat as pure gold! People who eat well have a glow to their skin and a bounce to their step. That's what I want!

10. Your body is a priority. Exercising isn't negotiable. There are no excuses. There are parks, websites, apps, videos, and gyms on every corner. Exercising isn't only important for weight loss, but muscle strength as well. My body confidence comes from how strong I feel.

11. Never deprive your body of food. Extreme dieting is so detrimental, and it doesn't feel good. You must love yourself first and always. Find nourishing, nurturing, and loving ways to manage your body. It's the only one you have.

Testimonials:

Georgette has taught me that it's okay to struggle with food and exercising; I've stopped beating myself up and now I focus on gentle ways to take care of myself. It's amazing how a simple shift in the way I think has helped me let go of a lot of my body issues. —Randi

I was extreme with my exercise and diet routine. I didn't realize it, but after reading Georgette's book, I have included yoga and deep breathing into my routine. I didn't realize how exhausted I was. Getting centered and calm has been wonderful. I feel better and my body has responded in kind. —Maryellen

11

Brilliant Money Ideas

"See yourself living in abundance and you will attract it. It always works. It works every time with every person."

Bob Proctor, author

1. Follow your heart. Although I will mention ways to conserve money, I am also encouraging you to DREAM BIG! I believe you can have it all. Financial advisor and motivational speaker, Suze Orman will be the first person to tell you to live within your means, but you can also set lofty financial goals; make specific goals with the specific dates you are going to meet them. Make a vision board with

all the beautiful material things you'd like to acquire. Feel how happy these beautiful items will make you. When I picture my family romping at our beach house or on vacation in Disney, the success permeates my being! I feel great! *Success Principles* by Jack Canfield will inspire you and help you create a path for wealth.

2. Read *It's Not About the Money*, by Bob Proctor and any book by Suze Orman—they have tons of great advice and eye-opening perspectives on how important it is to be positive as you pursue your passions with a clear vision. Reading and gathering information on finances is paramount to those of us who never discuss money in our homes and don't have any real financial sense.

3. Don't charge! If you can't pay for it, don't buy it. Credit cards lull us into believing that we have more money than we actually do. It's so easy to swipe that card, but if

you're paying in cash, you are touching the money and physically watching it leave your wallet. There's a lot more awareness when you pay in cash!

4. Avoid feeling like you're a victim if you can't afford something. Instead, be proud that you made the DECISION—you made a conscious choice about how to spend your money. You didn't let marketing, ads or social pressure dictate what comes out of your wallet. There's a lot of power and freedom in that.

5. There is a lot of adult peer pressure. People expect you to have the latest and greatest. Marketing has really gotten the best of us. Every year, car models change just enough, so we all know exactly how old everyone's car is. The same is true for smartphones and clothes. So many young people buy Louis Vuitton pocketbooks that cost more than their two-week paycheck! It's crazy how much pressure people feel, but mounting debt isn't the answer. We need to

be strong and secure in who we are without focusing all our attention on impressing other people. Read *The Millionaire Next Door* by Thomas J. Stanley to understand that many millionaires don't feel the need to flaunt their wealth. They would rather invest their money than lease expensive cars, buy status objects, or live in status neighborhoods.

6. Do you really need a second floor or a major renovation in your house? Several years ago, when all our neighbors were making major expansions, we decided to hold tight to our small home. We knew that our taxes would double, and we didn't want the extra payment. Today, our house is almost paid off and we don't have the stress and pressure of paying enormous mortgage and tax bills. The goal is to enjoy life, and stress is definitely a kill-joy!

7. When you retire, do you want a mass of bills? When you make financial decisions

that require years to pay the debt, you may want to reconsider your priorities. It may seem like a long way off, but speak with anyone who has retired. Time goes by quickly. You can't lose sight of the fact that you have to plan for your retirement.

8. Money management requires focus, discipline, prioritizing, and goal setting. For me, it also required a lot of reading and learning. We didn't discuss finances in my house when I was growing up, so I really didn't have great financial skills. I'm still working on this, and I probably always will. I like to be conscious of how *I choose* to save or spend money. Managing your money is time well spent.

9. There is an abundance of everything in the world. Can you even count the snowflakes during a snowstorm? Have you seen a field of flowers? How many blades of grass are in a park? We have to believe that abundance is our birthright and that this generous

world we live in will support all our needs as well.

10. Are you blocking yourself from abundance? If you are not living the financial lifestyle you want, reflect on your beliefs about money. What did your parents teach you? What does society say? I realized recently that I was carrying around the belief that, "Money is dirty." How could I possibly manifest financial abundance if I believe money is filthy?! Now I visualize money as clean and crisp linen sheets that smell great and protect me while I sleep. It makes me smile just to think of this! If you have any limiting beliefs, be diligent in changing them. Tell a new financial story. Every time you think of money, picture all the wonderful ways it will enhance your life. Empower yourself by knowing you can create the financial life you want.

11. Sometimes we stress out so much and hold on so tightly to our financial

woes, that we don't realize how much it interferes with our progress. This only builds negative momentum. When you feel the financial stress, breathe through it. Divert your attention to something pleasant. Have a couple of positive affirmations written somewhere that will ease the stress. "Abundance shows up in my life everywhere." "I am successful and prosperous." Find affirmations on websites or apps that speak to you personally. You'll know when you found the right affirmation because you'll feel better the minute you read it.

Testimonials:

Reading the chapter about money was difficult for me. I have been financially irresponsible my whole life. After reading the money chapter I can see how important it is to be aware of your beliefs around money. It has helped me set attainable financial goals. It makes me feel good to watch my bank account grow! —Suzanne

I read this chapter over and over again. Educating myself on finances has released a lot of stress for me and Georgette's book is an excellent resource. —Robert

11

to put their gross income on a post-it note on their fridge. Whenever I see the number, I smile! I build on that momentum of happiness.

3. When people are standing around gossiping—run the other way! Sometimes the gossip is so juicy, I'm mesmerized. My eyes glaze over like I'm staring at a wall of diamonds. It's addicting, but nothing good comes out of a group of people talking about someone. Sometimes as I walk away, I have to talk to myself, "Don't say anything. Don't listen. You don't want to know." Think of the 17 second momentum rule. If people are standing around speaking negatively about someone, consider how much momentum that builds and how much damage it can do. You don't want to be a part of that because you are focused on feeling confident and wonderful!

4. You may not like someone at work. You may really not like someone, but I promise you that if you go to a new job, that person's

Brilliant Career

"Wherever you go, there you are."

Jon Kabat-Zinn, author

Sometimes it just seems easier if you quit your job, but have you noticed that wherever you work, the same problems and situations show up?

1. When I focus on the positive aspects of my job, it allows me to concentrate on what I need to do to be successful, productive, dynamic, and extremely effective.

2. When things go wrong, and they do, I focus on something positive. When people complain to me about their job, I tell them

personality will show up in someone else! It's important that we learn to work with difficult people. Once we develop some tools and strategies, it gets easier. The first thing I've learned is that not everyone is going to like me. In the past, I would try really hard to befriend everyone. I was convinced that I could make cranky people like me. What a waste of my focus and energy! Even worse, my constant insistence on developing a relationship with these people would always backfire! Now I'm cordial, but I don't feel a need to bend over backwards for anyone. When I do feel the need to rush in, I take a deep breath and keep my distance. I establish and maintain respectable boundaries. It's hard because I want everyone to like me; I want to tell jokes and have everyone laugh, but it's much more important that I keep my dignity and confidence intact.

5. Don't take things personally. I believed that someone's behavior was a reflection of how

they felt about me. That seems so silly now. Everyone is fighting a battle that you know nothing about—it's actually pretty self-centered of us to assume we affect other's moods. Stay focused on how positive you are feeling and minimize the impact this person's mood is having on you. I like to visualize this person on a cloud drifting away. Whenever my thoughts drift back to how annoyed I feel, I put the person back on the cloud and let it drift away. Eventually, I will stop thinking about him/her.

6. The more you laser-beam focus on your career, the better you'll feel. Develop the skills needed to advance in your job. Continue to educate yourself. Make sure you're professionally dressed, on time, diligent in your job responsibilities, enthusiastic, motivated, and know the rules. If you don't, find a mentor at your job. Who's successful, happy, hardworking, and enthusiastic?! That's who you want to

emulate. So many leaders have said in their own words that, "Genius is attention to detail."

7. Make time to read and learn. I have read in many places that CEOs read 3-5 books a month, which enhances their success. Read about your industry, time management, and professionalism. Whatever your job is, be your best!

8. Network and stay marketable. Be aware of what other industries are doing, and stay on the cutting edge of your profession. Meet people who could potentially bolster your career. Just be careful your networking doesn't turn into a sloppy happy hour. Drinking and staying sharp don't mix well.

9. Always look for ways to advance and make more money. Financial independence is powerful!

10. I work with a woman who is extremely abrasive. She has no idea that she turns people off. If you can be aware and work

on some aspect of your personality that will enhance your abilities to communicate and work with people, go for it! Successful people know their strengths and weaknesses.

11. Avoid impulsively jumping into a romance at work. You make yourself so vulnerable. Do you really want someone you work with to know intimate details about you? Not only will your private life be exposed, but you risk losing the respect and reputation that make you so effective. Unfortunately, people will focus on your affair even after it's long over. It doesn't matter that you've worked hard for many years to build a stellar career. It's not easy to refrain when the feelings of heightened infatuation are calling you and you feel the longing. But in the long run, being in control of your actions will serve you best.

Testimonials:

I have been looking for a job for months. I was worried and anxious and losing hope when I came upon Georgette's book. Keeping the book on my kitchen counter, I refer to it before I send emails or make phone calls. Her message uplifted me and gave me patience and courage to persevere. Life is a journey. Now that I'm calm and can think clearly, so many creative ideas have come to me that I've turned into marketable opportunities. I now get that life has many options, and I am open to all that is wonderful and coming my way! —Erin

I've had a lot of jobs and I used to think that a new job was a fresh start with new people. Georgette's coaching has taught me that wherever you go, the same problems are always there. So I've stayed at my job and through Georgette's coaching, I have learned to talk to my boss and gossipy coworkers. I can see how you can't change people but you can learn how to work side by side with difficult people. —Noreen

11

Brilliant Child Rearing

"Your children are not your children.
They are the sons and daughters of
Life's longing for itself…"

Kahlil Gibran, Lebanese writer

1. Having a child is one of life's miracles, but nothing prepares you for child rearing! I wanted a family more than anything else in the world. It took me five years to conceive my son. Even so, I was not prepared for all the decisions I would have to make on his behalf or the awesome responsibility of keeping another human being healthy and alive. Breathe, enjoy the unfolding of watching your child grow, and trust that everything will be okay.

2. Ask for help. Moms feel tremendous guilt, but you are no good to anyone when you are exhausted. I liken it to, "I love chocolate, but I don't want to eat it 24 hours a day, 7 days a week." Everyone needs a break—if you are overwhelmed and exhausted, you've waited too long to ask for help.

3. Have fun! Smile! We get so serious about our responsibilities that we forget to enjoy our children and ourselves.

4. Children need balance. It would be so easy to let my son watch television or play video games all day long. It's like having a built in babysitter, but it is terribly irresponsible on our parts. Like Socrates said, "Everything in moderation, including moderation." My son balances video games with playing outside, walking the dog and other activities. He really gets that it's in his best interest to move.

5. Have clear boundaries and expectations of your children. Don't be afraid to enforce

your strong convictions. I expect respect. My son has a bedtime. I expect him to walk the dog and keep his room semi-neat. Does he challenge me? All the time, but I stick to my convictions.

6. When you make all the decisions for your child, you are making the statement, "You can't do this. You need me to do this for you." What's happening is that what may be acceptable for a 2-year-old, like mom putting the child's coat on, looks ridiculous when it involves an 17-year-old. I have seen mothers on a baseball field applying sunscreen on their 17-year-old sons' faces while these boys just stand there motionless. In our effort to protect our children, we've taken away their basic, normal, and natural abilities to grow, be independent, and assume responsibilities that come with age and experience. Just remember that we should be preparing them to live independently. So many parents today are doing their college children's homework

via email and, by constantly texting, they aren't even allowing their children to make decisions while they are away at school! This doesn't make you an awesome parent. You are crippling your child who can't grow because he/she isn't experiencing the normal growing pains that come with making decisions for yourself.

7. We are energetically connected to our children. If I'm tense about a situation, my son gets tense. If I'm upset about something, chances are, it will upset him too. I try to be calm and nonchalant when I know he is looking at me for validation. When he plays sports, I just smile at him. I'm not putting any meaning on matters that will come and go. These are his life's ups and downs, and I won't let my anxiety or disappointments affect his experiences and accomplishments.

8. It's okay for your child to feel pain. Why has this generation of parents put so much

emphasis on protecting their children from life's normal ups and downs? They are going to argue with friends. They are going to be excluded sometimes. A teacher is going to reprimand them. These life experiences hurt, but they also allow a child to figure out how to work through them. And when they work through their problems, they gain confidence and a maturity that can only come from reflecting on their behavior and being able to understand how their actions sometimes cause the problem. It is through adversity that we grow and become productive members of a family and community.

9. Adult peer pressure is brutal. Other parents can be condescending if you're not raising your children the exact same way they are—like there is a "right" way to do it. They have taken the natural process of parenting and created a horrific blueprint where parents are involved in every aspect of their children's lives, spending a lot of

time talking about the minutiae of child rearing. It makes it difficult if you have your own ideas about child rearing. You have to follow your gut, your own instincts, and intuition.

10. Breathe. Sometimes anxiety gets the best of us, but we don't have to live in so much fear. Yes, having children is an awesome responsibility and sad/horrible things do happen, but we can't live our lives anticipating every and any possible mishap. There is no joy in that, and we don't want to raise our children to be fearful.

11. Parenting takes consistency. For us, we are constantly encouraging our son to finish his homework (it's been eight years now!), and it gets old. Sometimes I want to give up because I'm tired, but I can't. He has to meet his responsibilities to become a productive, responsible, and confident adult. Our goals for our children should always start with the end in mind. We

need to make sure that we are giving them the skills to live on their own. Whether it's going away to college or living in their first apartment, our children will someday need to feed themselves, understand the constructs of working, managing money, washing clothes, etc. Our children's healthy independence is the ultimate sign of successful parenting.

Testimonials:

I thought I was being a great parent because I was my teenage son's dishwasher, personal cook, alarm clock, and washing machine! But he wasn't happy, and we were fighting all the time. Georgette helped me realize that I was smothering him. It hasn't been an easy transition for either of us, but I have to say, the house is calmer and we are getting along better because I am not following him around micromanaging him! —Melanie

11

Brilliant Breakups and Divorce

"We attract lovers from our level of energy... If you want to live happily ever after, learn to manage your emotions and make joy the most important experience. It's much more satisfying to get into a blissful place and attract a blissful person... than to be in a negative place and attract a negative person..."

Abraham Hicks

1. This may be a great time to reinvent yourself, make fun plans, or set new goals. Take the time to journal and reflect about what and who you would like to attract into your life. Cut your hair, lift weights, run a marathon, attend a function at an art

gallery, or travel somewhere exotic. Step out of your comfort zone, and have fun!

2. It's a great time to look for the loving support of family and friends, but don't overburden them by telling them the same stories over and over. You want to move your momentum away from depression and despair. The more you talk about the break up, the more you'll feel stuck. See a movie or go for a hike. Visit an aquarium or go to a concert. Distract yourself, and it will bring a little relief. The more you can do this, the better you will feel.

3. Don't drink or take drugs while you are healing from the pain of the relationship. You are not going to make wise decisions under the influence, and your ultimate goal is to come through this gracefully with your confidence and integrity intact. If you feel surges of anger towards your ex, that is normal. Resist the temptation to call or text in those vulnerable moments. They become lose-lose situations.

4. One of the best ways to heal is to be honest with yourself. Was this person really right for you? Were there things wrong with the relationship, but you put your blinders on because you were "in love"? Whenever I ask my clients this question, they sheepishly admit that there were indeed warning signs that they were ignoring. Being honest with yourself will help you heal. Minimally, if you feel surges of anger, you can pause and remember that you were aware of the person's shortcomings. This will help ease the anger you are harboring. Your ultimate goal is to release anger and bitterness, so you don't carry any negative emotions into your new life!

5. If you've neglected any aspect of your life—your friends, family, work, exercise, or hobbies—now is a great time to focus and nurture the parts of yourself that you love.

6. Don't sit inside brooding. Don't waste your time feeling victimized. Get outside! I used

to browse through Barnes and Noble. I loved walking all over a city and exploring. I used to hike with friends. Find activities that feel good, and get busy!

7. It may be too soon, but picture yourself with an ideal partner. Start putting out positive images to the universe. The first thing I would say is, "I want someone in my life who loves and supports me." Keep creating positive statements about the person you'd like to attract. I would focus most of my statements on the emotional and spiritual attributes you'd like in a person. Sometimes we think we want someone tall, dark, and handsome, but we forget to include the other really important qualities a person has to have like: kindness, honesty, integrity, loyalty, financial responsibility, etc.

8. Just keep moving. It's okay to feel sorry for yourself and to lie on the couch, but give yourself a deadline. I'll say, "Okay, I can lie here for 10 minutes and then I'm going to

get up and throw a load of wash in." Once I'm up, I'll probably straighten up the kitchen. Once I'm distracted, I feel better and I leave the house and find something constructive to do. I'll run errands, I'll meet a friend for coffee, and I feel so much better because I know I'm living instead of moping in the house.

9. It takes time. Sometimes it seems crazy that your world has just fallen apart but you are still expected to show up to work or any other obligations, especially when all you want to do is sleep and eat ice cream. Well-meaning friends are impatient and say, "Get over it already!" It's hard to hear, but there is some value in that message. You definitely want to take the time to heal, but you also want to make sure that you don't stop living.

10. Sometimes you need to be really gentle with yourself. Get a massage, take yoga classes, go to spiritual lectures, or take up

activities that are restorative and make you feel healthy and vital. People who take this approach to break ups come out healthier, centered, and ready to face the next chapter in their lives with clarity and hope.

11. I am a big proponent of therapy. If you see a pattern showing up in your life—you always date people who cheat or you let people take advantage of you—this is a good time to talk to a professional who can help you make better decisions about the people you allow in your life. It could be a wonderful opportunity to learn about yourself and attract someone who will enhance your life. That sounds exciting!

Testimonials:

I was in such a crazy cycle of texting horrible things to my ex all day long. We were constantly fighting even though we don't live together anymore. Georgette taught me that I need to let go of the relationship and that every time I texted her, I was keeping the marriage alive. Even though it felt great to criticize her through texts, I stopped. I am so glad I did. Now it seems so silly to me. I am focused on myself and my personal growth. I am back at the gym and

I lost 80 pounds! Letting go of the negativity has helped me reach for a happy life! —Jim

Georgette has helped me see that a breakup can be a fresh start. I spent years with someone in a bad relationship. We were always fighting, and I was always forgiving her unfaithfulness. Thanks to Georgette now I put myself first. I am very excited to meet someone new because I know I deserve to be happy. —Connie

11

Until We Meet Again...

Something magical happens when you put these practices into place. When you make yourself a priority, you find your voice! Taking action and setting boundaries has given me clarity to see how much I was in my own way. I have been working on these principles for many years. Some have been easy for me to implement, and others I am still working on today. It takes time to change habits that have been instilled in me from childhood, and I get a lot of satisfaction watching myself grow. For all of this to work in a meaningful and positive way that moves you to the life you want, you have to *practice* thinking happy thoughts. You will have to be *patient* with yourself because some days this will be difficult, but you will practice yourself into a good place again. You will be *persistent* because, for some of us, it takes time. Be gentle and kind with yourself as you grow. And *persevere*, because you will be practicing this new you forever. Once you've practiced yourself into feeling good, you will want to reach for those wonderful feelings every day. As you do this, beautiful new habits and thoughts will emerge, and love, joy, and abundance will flow into your life naturally.

Some people get faster results than me, but I don't judge because it's not a competition. All that matters is that I'm working on it! I'm working on being more efficient when I know a principle will support my success. I'm working on releasing resistance so that I can fulfill my dreams. You know you are in a pattern of resistance when someone tells you something like, "You could have handled that situation better," and one of the first words out of your mouth includes the word ***but***. The minute you say, "***But***," you are justifying and explaining and digging in your heels. You are not receptive to the message or the change that needs to occur; you are resisting. For me, resistance comes loud and clear when I don't even begin a project or I procrastinate and don't finish something when sometimes all that's required is an email or a phone call. Whenever I don't do something that I want to do, I know there's resistance there. I work on letting it go. Sometimes I take baby steps with a project if I feel overwhelmed. Sometimes I find if I start something, the resistance goes away and I can accomplish one of my goals. Resistance does not allow for growth or expansion. It puts you out of the flow of life. That's why it's so important to be flexible and open to new ideas, possibilities, and change. You can't change a pattern or a problem if you are resisting the solutions.

And when life has its bumps, focus on what you do well. Focus on what is going right in your life. Focus on the fullness of your life so that part of you grows. Focus on your spouse's good qualities. Think of all the wonderful things your child does well. If you are smiling, you are not frowning! If you're feeling good, you've given yourself a moment of relief. Keep building those moments so they turn into hours, days, weeks, months, and years of joy! You can create a happy life!

You are worthy and lucky. Positive works for everyone—no exceptions. If your life is clouded by problems, clear away the layers. If you worry about things like what your neighbors or other people think, you are giving your power away. You are using all of your energy to deal with these situations, and you are not leaving anything for yourself. You are focusing on things that can't change. If you stopped doing that and stopped being upset, angry, and moody over these issues and situations, you would have a vast amount of time and energy to be brilliant. It isn't easy to let go, but, when you do, you are free. You will never go back there again. I never want to waste a minute of energy on someone who cuts me off in a car or on a friend, relative, or coworker who is rude and disrespectful. If someone is angry or moody, I don't own it. It's totally on that person. I refuse to take part in those transactions. As a matter of fact, I've declared out loud, "No one is allowed to be mad at me." It works! I have never felt better about myself in my life. I finally understand that this freedom is the core of allowing.

Although I'm working hard on my own, this book and my growth were enhanced by my wonderful therapist/life coach, Cheryl Worzala. We are a team. I enjoy the safety of her office as we discuss and make weekly plans that make me present to my growth. It is important when you are sitting with a therapist that you feel you have a partner in your process. Growth is developmental—enjoy building a relationship with yourself. It's a gift and the key to successful transformation. Another important key is that therapy takes time. I am proud of myself because I have been in the process for a long time. For some people, there may be a stigma to therapy, but I now know that if I want to heal and grow, having a talented therapist helps tremendously. I am incredibly grateful for the support Cheryl has provided.

Caring positive friends are also key. We support one another all the time in our quest for joy. I highly recommend that you read this book with a couple of friends who are on the same path and are committed to living a positive and fulfilling life.

The ideas in this book are simple and approachable. It's all in your perception. If you get frustrated by life's daily ups and downs (which never go away), it will be difficult for you to see clearly enough to focus on a solution. Sometimes we get so stuck—whether it's our cultural or family of origin's perceptions—that it's hard for us to try something new or to even believe that there is another way to accomplish a goal or a dream. Once you become open to the possibilities, you will see that there are thousands of ways to approach a problem, a project, life—keep trying new things until something works for you. Hopefully your newfound skills will help you navigate issues quickly and efficiently so you can confidently build a life you love.

11

Brilliant Resources

"Not all readers are leaders,
but all leaders are readers."

Harry Truman,
33rd President of the United States

Reading is a daily reminder to live a life that brings you joy. Wonderful, nurturing books, authors, websites, and blogs:

www.georgettevanvliet.com
Esther and Jerry Hicks
www.abraham-hicks.com
Wayne Dyer
Louise Hay
Bob Proctor
Jack Canfield
Julia Cameron
Suze Orman
Joe Vitale
Gabrielle Bernstein
Pam Grout
Cheryl Worzala

11

Glossary of Terms

1. Abraham-Hicks—Esther Hicks is an inspirational speaker and author. She delivers messages through a group of spiritually evolved teachers known as Abraham. Go to the website www.abraham-hicks.com for more information.

2. Law of Attraction—the first of the three Eternal Universal Laws that Abraham teachers (Read The *Law of Attraction, The Basics of the Teachings of Abraham*, both by Esther and Jerry Hicks). The most powerful law in the Universe is, "That which is like unto itself is drawn." Whatever you think about, whether positive or negative, you draw into your life. You are the inviter, the

creator, and the attractor of all the things that have come to you.

3. Asking, Believing, Receiving—the basic theory of Law of Attraction: ask specifically for what you want, believe with all your heart that you can have what you want, and be open to receiving your desires.

4. Manifesting—to make your dreams a reality. To manifest your desires, have a clear image of what you want. Your words are key—be aware of what you speak because you manifest what you are thinking and speaking.

5. Ease down—to stop what you are doing if you're stressed, anxious, or exhausted. You quiet your mind and think sweet thoughts. You breathe. You meditate. You do whatever you need to do to feel relaxed and centered.

6. Momentum—If you can hold a thought for 17 seconds without being distracted or contradicting it, you have started the

process of manifestation. If you hold your thought for 17...34...51...68 seconds, what you desire will start to make its way into your life. As quickly as 68 seconds, and you have given birth to a manifestation. Be careful that this momentum is positive! It can also go in the other direction. If I spend 68 seconds focusing on the wonderful aspects of my marriage, I smile and feel love. If I focus on the negative aspects, I'm angry and frustrated. If I focus 68 seconds on the aspects of my job that I love, I feel successful and gratified. If I focus on the negative, I'll feel miserable. Directing your thoughts really can be the difference between a wonderful or a depressing day!

11